UNITED STATES BY REGION

People and Places of the
SOUTHEAST
by John Micklos, Jr.

Consultant:
Dr. David Lanegran
John S. Holl Professor of Geography
Macalester College
St. Paul, Minnesota

CAPSTONE PRESS
a capstone imprint

Fact Finders Books are published by Capstone Press,
1710 Roe Crest Drive, North Mankato, Minnesota 56003
www.mycapstone.com

Copyright © 2017 by Capstone Press, a Capstone imprint. All rights reserved. No part of this publication may be reproduced in whole or in part, or stored in a retrieval system, or transmitted in any form or by any means, electronic, mechanical, photocopying, recording, or otherwise, without written permission of the publisher.

Library of Congress Cataloging-in-Publication Data
Names: Micklos, John, author.
Title: People and places of the Southeast / by John Micklos, Jr.
Description: North Mankato, Minnesota : Capstone Press, [2017] | Includes bibliographical references and index. | Audience: Grades 4–6.
Identifiers: LCCN 2016008967 | ISBN 9781515724438 (library binding) | ISBN 9781515724483 (pbk.) | ISBN 9781515724537 (ebook : pdf)
Subjects: LCSH: Southern States—Juvenile literature.
Classification: LCC F209.3 .M53 2017 | DDC 975—dc23
LC record available at https://lccn.loc.gov/2016008967

Editorial Credits
Angie Kaelberer, editor; Cynthia Della-Rovere, designer; Svetlana Zhurkin, media researcher; Laura Manthe, production specialist

Photo Credits
Alamy: John Zada, 25; Dreamstime: Ddmitr, 16; FEMA: Jocelyn Augustino, 17; iStockphoto: Beachcottage Photography, 27; Library of Congress, 13 (bottom); Newscom: Glasshouse Images, 8, UPI Photo Service, 13 (top); North Wind Picture Archives, 10–11; Shutterstock: Andrew B. Hall, 21, Fotoluminate LLC, cover (bottom), Linda Moon, 22–23, Mark Van Dyke Photography, 6, 15, Morphart Creation, 9, Olesia Bilkei, cover (top), Stacie Stauff Smith Photos, 28, Todd Castor, 19

Design and Map Elements by Shutterstock

Table of Contents

Introduction 4
Chapter 1: People and History 8
Chapter 2: Land and Climate 14
Chapter 3: Economy 20
Chapter 4: Daily Life and Culture 26

Glossary 30
Read More 31
Internet Sites 31
Index 32

Introduction

Crispy Southern fried chicken and spicy Cajun food are dishes you'll find in the Southeast. You'll hear bluegrass and jazz music. You'll visit small towns and bustling cities. In the distance are the Appalachian Mountains, sandy beaches, and the mighty Mississippi River. The Southeast region of the United States is a place where different elements blend into one.

The Southeast has a rich **ethnic** heritage. Just as an example, many people in Louisiana have a mix of French, Spanish, and African or American Indian ancestry.

> **ethnic:** relating to a group of people sharing the same national origins, language, or culture

The region includes 14 states and the District of Columbia. Florida, Georgia, and North Carolina are among the nation's most populated states. But Delaware and the District of Columbia are among U.S. areas with the lowest populations. Southeast states with average populations are Maryland, West Virginia, Virginia, Kentucky, Tennessee, South Carolina, Arkansas, Louisiana, Mississippi, and Alabama.

The Southeast Region by Rank

A lot of people enjoy living in the Southeast. In fact Florida is one of the most popular states to live in the nation. Let's take a look at each state or area as it compares to the others in the region. This chart also includes information on each state's size, capital, and nickname.

South Carolina is called the Palmetto State for its state tree, the palmetto.

State or Area	Population	Rank	Square Miles	Rank	Capital	Nickname
Alabama	4,849,377	23	52,423	30	Montgomery	Yellowhammer State
Arkansas	2,966,369	32	53,182	28	Little Rock	Natural State
Delaware	935,614	45	2,489	49	Dover	First State
District of Columbia	658,893	49	68	51	None	None official
Florida	19,893,297	3	59,988	23	Tallahassee	Sunshine State
Georgia	10,097,343	8	59,441	24	Atlanta	Peach State
Kentucky	4,413,457	26	40,411	37	Frankfort	Bluegrass State
Louisiana	4,649,676	25	51,843	31	Baton Rouge	Pelican State
Maryland	5,976,407	19	12,407	42	Annapolis	Old Line State
Mississippi	2,992,333	31	48,434	32	Jackson	Magnolia State
North Carolina	9,943,964	9	52,672	29	Raleigh	Tar Heel State
South Carolina	4,832,482	24	32,007	40	Columbia	Palmetto State
Tennessee	6,549,352	17	42,146	36	Nashville	Volunteer State
Virginia	8,326,289	12	42,769	35	Richmond	Old Dominion State
West Virginia	1,850,326	38	24,231	41	Charleston	Mountain State

Chapter 1

People and History

The Southeast was one of the first parts of North America explored by Europeans. Spanish explorers reached Florida in the early 1500s. In 1607 the English started a settlement at Jamestown, Virginia. It was the first permanent English settlement in the area. Wherever they landed Europeans found American Indian cultures already there. Major tribes included the Cherokee, Chickasaw, Choctaw, and Seminole.

Jamestown, Virginia, was the first permanent settlement in the New World.

Sequoyah

Few American Indian tribes had written languages. Their histories were passed down through spoken stories. In the early 1800s a Cherokee man named Sequoyah decided to create a Cherokee alphabet. He spent many years creating symbols for the sounds that made up Cherokee words. His system was easy to learn. Within months, many members of the Cherokee Nation could read using Sequoyah's alphabet.

As more settlers came to the Southeast, American Indians faced tough choices. The Seminole fought to hold onto their land in Florida. They battled for more than 40 years. In the end the U.S. government forced most Seminole to move to Oklahoma. Other tribes were pressured into signing treaties that took away their lands. In 1838 the Cherokee were forced to walk to Oklahoma. About 4,000 died of hunger and disease along the way. Their march is known as the Trail of Tears.

Historical Importance

The Southeast has played a major role throughout U.S. history. Many Revolutionary War leaders were from Virginia. Four of the nation's first five presidents also came from that state.

In the 1700s and 1800s, farming was big business in the Southeast. Some farmers owned large **plantations** that grew cotton, rice, and other crops. Black people were brought from Africa and made to work as slaves. For years Northern and Southern states argued over slavery. Some Northerners believed slavery should be against the law. People in Southern states disagreed. They said states should have the right to make their own laws.

African-Americans were made to work as slaves on plantations. They loaded rice on barges in South Carolina.

plantation: a large farm where crops such as cotton and sugarcane are grown

Slavery was one of the issues that led to the Civil War (1861–1865). In 1861, 11 states **seceded** from the Union to create the Confederate States of America. These included most of the southeastern states. Kentucky, Maryland, and Delaware remained in the Union. Virginia seceded but people in the western part of the state disagreed with that decision. They formed the new state of West Virginia. Washington, D.C., was home to the Union capital. This area is between Virginia and Maryland. The Confederate capital was less than 100 miles (160 kilometers) away in Richmond, Virginia.

secede: to formally withdraw from a group or organization, often to form another group

Nearly all of the war's battles were fought on Southern soil. Many areas suffered damage. When the Civil War ended in 1865, slavery ended as well. After the war, the former Confederate states underwent a painful period of **Reconstruction.**

African-Americans continued to face many challenges. Many Southern states passed laws to keep them from voting, attending good schools, and holding well-paying jobs. In the 1950s and 1960s, Dr. Martin Luther King Jr. and others led the **civil rights** movement. The Civil Rights Act in 1964 gave African-Americans equal rights. But they still face **discrimination** in some places.

The Southeast also had a boom in industry during the 1900s. Atlanta and other large cities grew rapidly. With its warm, sunny climate, Florida's population greatly increased. It attracted large numbers of Spanish-speaking immigrants from Central and South America. Many retired people also moved to Florida to leave behind the cold northern winters. In recent years, the Southeast and the West have been the fastest-growing U.S. regions.

Reconstruction: the period of time following the Civil War, when the U.S. government tried to rebuild Southern states

civil rights: the rights that all people have to freedom and equal treatment under the law

discrimination: unfair treatment of a person or group, often because of race, religion, or gender

On August 28, 1963, Dr. Martin Luther King Jr. delivered his famous "I Have a Dream" speech. His work helped to give African-Americans equal rights.

Harriet Tubman

Born a slave in Maryland in 1822, Harriet Tubman escaped to freedom in 1849. Then she worked on the Underground Railroad. She made nearly 20 trips into slave territory to lead hundreds of other slaves to freedom. During the Civil War she served as a nurse, scout, and spy for the Union.

Chapter 2
Land and Climate

Deep rivers and high mountains are found throughout the Southeast. At 300 to 500 million years old, the Appalachians are the oldest mountain range in North America. The range begins in Alabama and ends in Maine. The famous Appalachian Trail covers 2,185 miles (3,516 km) and starts in Georgia. It winds through North Carolina, Tennessee, Virginia, West Virginia, and Maryland. It then enters the Northeast region and ends in Maine.

At 2,340 miles (3,766 km), the Mississippi River is the second-longest U.S. river. It touches Kentucky, Tennessee, Arkansas, Mississippi, and Louisiana. Then it empties into the Gulf of Mexico. The Mississippi River has been a major shipping route since the early 1800s. Other major rivers flowing through the Southeast include the Ohio and Tennessee.

FACT

The Mississippi River's name comes from several American Indian languages. Common translations are "ancient river" or "ancient father of waters."

The Blue Ridge Mountains can be found along the Appalachian Trail.

Climate

Temperatures can be warm in the Southeast during much of the year. States in the northern part of the region, such as Delaware and Maryland, have milder temperatures. Monthly average high temperatures range from 42 degrees to 89 degrees Fahrenheit (6 to 32 degrees Celsius). Farther south, the climate gets warmer. Several states have average monthly temperatures of more than 75°F (24°C) during the summer.

The region also receives a lot of rain. With 60 inches (150 centimeters) each year, Louisiana is the second-wettest state. All that moisture means that the air is very **humid**. New Orleans is one of the most humid U.S. cities.

With its warm weather, the Key West Promenade can be a fun place to visit.

humid: damp or moist

Southeastern states along the Gulf of Mexico and the Atlantic coast often experience **hurricanes**. On average about 10 Atlantic storms each year are major enough to earn names. About six reach hurricane strength, with wind speeds of 74 miles (119 km) per hour or higher.

Hurricane Katrina

Hurricane Katrina reached land in Louisiana on August 29, 2005. At that time it was a Category 3 hurricane, with winds reaching 140 miles (225 km) per hour. Hundreds of thousands of people in Louisiana, Mississippi, and Alabama had to leave their homes. Many **levees** in New Orleans failed, causing massive flooding. The storm killed at least 1,245 people and caused more than $100 billion in damage.

hurricane: a very large storm with high winds and rain; hurricanes form over warm ocean water

levee: an embankment built to prevent a body of water from overflowing

Animals and Plants

The Southeast's warm, moist climate supports a rich variety of plants and animals. The alligator has been around for 150 million years. Alligators grow up to 15 feet (5 meters) in length and can weigh 1,000 pounds (454 kilograms). They rarely attack humans, but their massive jaws and sharp teeth encourage people to stay away.

The warm climate also makes the region a perfect home for snakes. These include poisonous snakes, such as the cottonmouth, copperhead, and Eastern diamondback rattlesnake. In recent years, pythons were brought to Florida as pets. Some escaped or were released into the wild, where their numbers have grown.

Common trees in the Southeast include pine, magnolia, oak, and cypress. Palm trees also grow in much of Florida.

FACT

The Everglades National Park in Florida covers more than 1.5 million acres (607,029 hectares). More than 1 million people visit the park each year.

Alligators live in the swamps of the Florida Everglades.

Chapter 3
Economy

Many rural southeasterners are farmers. The soil and warm, moist climate are perfect for growing crops, such as cotton, soybeans, and corn. Many farmers in North Carolina raise livestock, such as poultry and hogs. Georgia grows peanuts and peaches. Its nickname is "The Peach State." Florida grows citrus fruits, such as grapefruit and oranges. Its orchards produce much of the nation's citrus crop.

Coal mining, which helps provide the nation's energy, is also important in many southeastern states. West Virginia and Kentucky rank among the nation's top three states in coal production. Together they produce 20 percent of the nation's coal.

Fishing is also a major industry in the Southeast. Louisiana and Virginia are among the nation's top five states in seafood catches. The region also has four of the nation's 10 busiest seaports.

Washington, D.C., is the seat of the federal government. That makes it a major employer. Its most famous employee is the president of the United States!

Fishing for shrimp in the Gulf of Mexico is very common.

Technology and Tourism

Many advances started in the Southeast. The Kennedy Space Center in Florida is the center of the U.S. space program. The moon exploration missions launched from there. So did the space shuttles.

In 1959 North Carolina established Research Triangle Park (RTP) to attract **research** facilities and industries to the state. More than 150 technology companies are located there. Cummings Research Park near Huntsville, Alabama, is another large research facility.

People can visit the NASA Kennedy Space Center Museum to learn about missions to space.

research: to study and learn about a subject

FACT

Research Triangle Park is North America's largest high-technology research and science park. It gets its name from its location between three cities: Durham, Chapel Hill, and Raleigh.

The Southeast is also a popular place to visit. Tourism is a major industry in the region. Florida ranks as one of the world's top tourist sites. In 2014 97 million tourists visited the state. Some come for the theme parks and attractions. Others come to enjoy the warm weather. More than 1 million people in the state work in the tourist industry!

Transportation

The Southeast includes a mixture of major highways and winding country roads. People can drive on six of the nation's 10 longest interstate highways. At nearly 2,000 miles (3,200 km), I-95 runs through seven southeastern states and the District of Columbia.

People can also visit nine of the 10 longest U.S. bridges in the Southeast. These include the 23-mile (37-km) Chesapeake Bay Bridge-Tunnel in Virginia. Its roads, bridges, and underwater tunnels allow motorists to cross the Chesapeake Bay. The nation's longest bridge, the Lake Pontchartrain Causeway in Louisiana, covers nearly 24 miles (38 km)!

People driving south on the Lake Pontchartrain Causeway will see New Orleans, Louisiana, in the distance.

Chapter 4

Daily Life and Culture

Many people consider the Southeast a rural region. But it's become more urban over time. Large cities include Washington, D.C.; Baltimore, Maryland; Jacksonville, Florida; Memphis, Tennessee; and Charlotte, North Carolina. Other major cities are Atlanta, Georgia; and Miami, Tampa, and Orlando in Florida.

In addition to big cities, the Southeast has many interesting small towns. They include Sevierville, Tennessee; St. Simons Island, Georgia; and Edenton, North Carolina. Sevierville is located in the foothills of the Great Smoky Mountains. Visitors there can explore the caves of the Forbidden Caverns. St. Simons Island is famous for beaches and sea wildlife. Edenton is known for its restored historic buildings dating from the early 1700s.

People who live in the rural Appalachian Mountains have a culture all their own. Traditions passed down through the centuries remain strong. These include storytelling, quilting, and bluegrass music featuring the banjo and fiddle.

Many visitors to St. Simons Island, Georgia, enjoy the beaches and fishing.

Fun in the Southeast

The Southeast is home to many historical sites. Virginia visitors tour Jamestown, Colonial Williamsburg, and President George Washington's home at Mount Vernon. Civil War battlefield sites dot the region's landscape. Another famous site is Kitty Hawk in North Carolina. This is where Orville and Wilbur Wright made the first airplane flight in 1903.

Visitors can see what life was like long ago in Colonial Williamsburg, Virginia.

> **FACT**
>
> Louis Armstrong was one of the best jazz musicians of all time. He was born in New Orleans in 1901. Armstrong's trumpet-playing skills earned him worldwide fame. His famous songs include "Hello, Dolly" and "What a Wonderful World."

Visitors to the Southeast will find much to keep them busy. Washington, D.C., offers museums, art galleries, and monuments, such as the Lincoln Memorial as well as the Vietnam War Memorial. The White House attracts more than 100,000 visitors each month.

Fans of all types of music come to the Southeast too. Nashville, Tennessee, is the capital of country music. It earned the nickname "Music City." Memphis, Tennessee, has Graceland. This is the home of rock-and-roll singer Elvis Presley. New Orleans is famous as the birthplace of jazz.

Orlando, Florida, is a top tourist spot. Its many theme parks include SeaWorld, Universal Studios, and Disney World. Disney World's Magic Kingdom is the world's most popular theme park.

Rich in both history and current attractions, the Southeast has much to offer. Both visitors and residents enjoy its many charms.

Glossary

civil rights (SI-vil RYTS)—the rights that all people have to freedom and equal treatment under the law

discrimination (dis-kri-muh-NAY-shuhn)—unfair treatment of a person or group, often because of race, religion, or gender

ethnic (ETH-nik)—relating to a group of people sharing the same national origins, language, or culture

humid (HYOO-mid)—damp or moist

hurricane (HUR-uh-kane)—a very large storm with high winds and rain; hurricanes form over warm ocean water

levee (LEV-ee)—an embankment built to prevent a body of water from overflowing

plantation (plan-TAY-shuhn)—a large farm where crops such as cotton and sugarcane are grown

Reconstruction (ree-kuhn-STRUHKT-shuhn)—the period of time following the Civil War, when the U.S. government tried to rebuild Southern states

research (REE-surch)—to study and learn about a subject

secede (si-SEED)—to formally withdraw from a group or an organization, often to form another organization

Read More

Felix, Rebecca. *The Southeast.* Regions of the U.S.A. Mankato, Minn: Child's World, 2013.

Hyde, Natalie. *What's in the Southeast?* All around the U.S. New York: Crabtree Pub., 2012.

Rau, Dana Meachen. *The Southeast.* A True Book. New York: Children's Press, 2012.

Santella, Andrew. *Southeast Indians.* First Nations of North America. Chicago: Heinemann Library, 2012.

Internet Sites

FactHound offers a safe, fun way to find Internet sites related to this book. All of the sites on FactHound have been researched by our staff.

Here's all you do:

Visit www.facthound.com

Type in this code: 9781515724438

Check out projects, games and lots more at
www.capstonekids.com

Index

American Indians, 4, 8, 9
   Sequoyah, 9
   Trail of Tears, 9

animals, 11, 18

Appalachian Mountains, 4, 27

Appalachian Trail, 14

Armstrong, Louis, 29

cities, 4, 12, 16, 23, 26

civil rights, 12

Civil War, 11, 12, 13, 28

climate, 12, 16, 18, 20
   rain, 16
   temperatures, 16

Confederate states, 11, 12

farms, 10, 20

fishing, 20

food, 4

Gulf of Mexico, 14, 17

hurricanes, 17

industry, 12, 20, 23

Jamestown, Virginia, 8, 28

Kennedy Space Center, 22

King, Martin Luther, Jr., 12

mining, 20

music, 4, 27, 29

plants, 18

Reconstruction, 12

Research Triangle Park, 22, 23

Revolutionary War, 10

rivers, 14
   Mississippi River, 4, 14, 15
   Ohio River, 14
   Tennessee River, 14

slavery, 10, 11, 12

tourism, 23, 29

transportation, 24

Tubman, Harriet, 13

Wright, Orville and Wilbur, 28